Copyright *Flora*

Julia Clements is President of the London and Overseas Flower Arrangement Association and Life Vice-President of the National Association of Flower Arrangement Societies.

Julia Clements is known and loved throughout the world for the joy she brings to so many people through her talks and demonstrations on flower arranging. She is the Founder of the Modern School of Floral Art and was awarded the Victoria Medal of Honour, the highest award of the Royal Horticultural Society, for her pioneer work in Flower Arranging. It is to her that we owe the phenomenal growth of flower arrangement clubs throughout the country, which have created a new domestic art and interest.

Here is a much welcomed picture book of flower arrangements by Julia Clements which will be an inspiration to the millions of people interested in flowers. Whether they wish to make a first attempt or whether they are confirmed flower arrangers, everyone will gain something by looking at the beauty of all the different types of arrangement from the formal and traditional to the stark modern style. The personal approach of the introduction, which also gives tips on the care of fresh flowers, together with the specially taken photographs, make up into a book to be enjoyed and treasured by all.

64 pages
24 black and white photographs
24 colour plates

A BATSFORD BOOK

JULIA CLEMENTS' FLOWER ARRANGEMENTS

B. T. Batsford Ltd
London

Arrangements by Julia Clements
Photographs by Jon Whitbourne

Frontispiece This formal mass display is made of summer flowers from the garden. Delphiniums, larkspur and hosta flowers form the outline, whilst paeonies strengthen the centre. Pinks, yellow achillia and *Alchemilla mollis* and scabious help to fill in with deutzia and escalonnia flowing downwards

3893897

© Julia Clements 1976
First published 1976
Reprinted 1981, 1982
ISBN 0 7134 32462

Printed in Hong Kong
for the publishers
B T Batsford Limited
4 Fitzhardinge Street
London WIH OAH

Overleaf   A twig of ivy and three yellow
chrysanthemums are held by a pinholder
in a tall pale blue cylinder type container.
A brown piece of root continues the
downward curve and gives weight at the
right

Introduction

This is a picture book of flower arrangements. Some you may like, others might not be your style. Some may appeal to you horticulturally, whilst others would not fit into your home setting. You may love the colouring of some of the arrangements yet abhor that of others. But they are all made for a reason; a reason which may evoke something in your own mind. And if you love arranging flowers it is by gazing at other arrangements, other colour schemes, other styles, that you eventually discover what you really want to do yourself.

Many people tell me that they would love to be able to arrange flowers but add that they can't even draw a straight line, let alone make a design with flowers. Others say they know nothing about plants and flowers.

Well, let nothing of this deter you. You cannot know it all at once, but you *can* make a *start* at once, and it is only by physically making the start can you discover how very easy it all is.

I recently met an attractive woman who said 'I love to see flowers beautifully arranged but I haven't a clue how to start'. She admitted she had never tried. We arranged that she bought a bunch of flowers the next day (we were staying in a hotel) and I encouraged her to cut the stems to different lengths, rather than have all the flower heads standing together at the top. In this way you could see the individual flowers and, by adding a few leaves, a different form was introduced. She had made the start and she was pleased; and then the questions started to flow. The barrier had been overcome.

Most of us want to make our homes more beautiful, and when entertaining friends we love to create a pleasing setting with flowers. Well, do remember if you *want* to arrange flowers artistically you can. There is no mystery about it and it need not take up a lot of time, nor cost you a lot of money. It depends upon what you want, or for what reason you are going to display your flowers.

On some special occasion you may want to create an impact with a large formal display of flowers. Another time you may just want to place a few flowers at the base of a bare branch in a shallow dish. For a dinner party you may wish to create a long low design in a colour scheme to match your china, or even place a few anemones in a pottery jar, but whatever you do must be right for you at the moment.

I meet many women in my travels all over Britain and in other parts of the

This exquisite dry arrangement of honesty, statice (sea lavender) and pink acrocliniums, all grown from seed, is made in a turquoise blue glass container. Stems held by floral foam

world who tell me that they long to do something creative, something by which they can express themselves. It may be the children have grown up, and she finds herself not needed so much, or bereaved and left alone, or prehaps retired with more time on her hands. It is true we all possess a certain amount of creative ability within us and long for an outlet, but few of us can find an immediate answer. Many creative pursuits take too long to give an answer at the time we need it, but with flower arranging it is different. Whether you have a big or small garden or none at all you could walk down a country lane or in the woods and find the basic material with which to make a living picture. And what is more, you can see the result almost at once. Then, when someone walks into the room and notices what you have done, you feel a great sense of satisfaction. And of course the subject is never-ending in interest and fascination, for the seasons are always changing, different varieties of flowers are there to be tried, as well as different colour schemes and soon you develop a 'seeing eye' which will lead you to all sorts of discoveries. When in the country you will 'see' chunky pieces of wood which might cover your pinholder in a shallow dish, yet previously you might not have noticed them. You will discover the beautiful movement of a twisty branch which might give height to a modern design. You will notice the form of large leaves that will give depth to a large arrangement or the delicacy of ferns that will outline a dainty table decoration. It will not stop there of course, for even at the seaside your eyes will be open for colourful stones or pieces of rock that can give stability low down in many new style arrangements. Shells too can be incorporated and even used as containers. The more your eyes are opened, the more exciting it all becomes. You will be led into 'seeing' vases or containers with new eyes. Of course you had seen them before but now you will be looking at texture, shape and colour in order that they may suit your flowers.

Many people have told me that a whole new world has been opened up before them through flower arranging. They have grown plants, they never knew the value of before, and tried others that will give a different or individual touch to their design. They have made friends at flower clubs and shows, church flower festivals and other artistic events. In fact one lady said that it is all becoming so interesting, that she now gets through her house chores in half the time which leaves her more free to visit shows and attend meetings.

A bare branch sprayed with gold paint gives height to this simple arrangement of green yew and pine cones held on a pinholder in a tin of water on a wooden base. The wooden deer was similarly painted

FLOWERS FROM SEEDS

Of course those with gardens are lucky, for you can even grow your own colour schemes. Just think of the miracle that comes from a packet of seeds. I get as much enjoyment in the winter from reading a seed catalogue as I do by reading a novel. I look at the height that the flowers will grow and their colours so that I am sure of some tall flowers and others shorter for low down in my arrangements and I always grow some ornamental grasses as well as trying something unusual every year.

I mention here some of the flowers I grow from seed, but if you are new to gardening, do follow the instructions on the seed packet for so many people, anxious for quick results sow the seed too early—you shold wait until the soil warms up in late spring.

Do try some pink larkspur and crimson godetia. Green love-lies-bleeding (*Amaranthus viridis*) gives an elegant touch in the autumn, other green flowers are zinnia 'envy' and nicotiana. Pink chiffon poppies are like crushed silk in an arrangement and a new crimson astor, called Amore Red, with six and more flowers to a stem makes a striking display for the table. Many others can be grown from seed, but the fun is in choosing for yourself from the catalogues. If you have the space I do advise you to sow a lot of your seed separately from the garden proper, so that you can pick for house decoration without spoiling the outdoor effect.

You will, I am sure also grow a number of perennial flowers if you do not already, flowers such as delphiniums, heleniums, golden rod, and achillia. These are the flowers that die down each year and come up again the next, but the flower arranger's greatest need at all times of the year is leaves. If you are in a hurry, some annual leaves can be grown from seed. Leaves such as zea maize, onopordon thistle will give you a result two months after sowing the seed. But a much better plan is to plant some evergreens, then you can cut from them all the year round.

Fortunately, evergreens last a long time when cut, so you will not have to denude the bushes, in fact one of the longest lasting in water is *Choisya ternata*. This is a beautiful shrub giving shiny green rosettes of leaves, so useful for tucking in to fill bare spaces, and in addition it has at times attractive white blossom. Another which comes into this category is *Viburnum tinus*. It has darker non-shiny leaves and again gives plentiful blossom in winter. Then I love the shrub *Aucuba*. It is commonly

known as spotted laurel, but the leaves give a bright splash when combined with winter flowers, and are so useful with the early daffodils. Another useful evergreen shrub is *Skimmia.* For many modern designs large cut leaves are most effective. If you have space, do plant some hostas. These will give large flat leaves from spring onwards, but will die down in winter. As if taking over in winter, the *Arum italicum* leaves start to appear and these die down in summer. *Bergenia cordifolia* is another plant giving large leathery-like leaves all the year round, which I find most useful in many designs, and I must not forget the fatzia japonica which has large lobed leaves often used in the stark modern arrangements. All of these different plants with their various sizes and textures will lead you to study catalogues and encourage you to visit flower shows where you can see these plants displayed.

Another good source of delight and knowledge is to visit gardens open to the public, you can then see the plants in their garden positions, and if you want to cover the whole range of flowers, plants, shrubs, roses, bulbs, in fact everything you could ever dream of, you can do not better than to visit regularly the Royal Horticultural Society's gardens at Wisley, near Ripley in Surrey.

LIVING IN TOWNS

When I am speaking or teaching often someone in the audience will say 'It's alright for those who have a garden, but I live in a flat in town'. Admittedly it is not quite so easy for those in towns, but it is far more challenging, I have always felt that obstacles are there to be overcome, so if you live in a town, why not take a trip now and again to the country. Breathe deeply the lovely clean air, and open your eyes to all that is around you. Take a small saw with you, for you are sure to come across an upturned tree that will provide you with lots of branches of interesting shapes and twisty roots. Chunks of moss-covered tree bark are also valuable finds, tree ivy, ferns, greenery, stones; in fact all kinds of long lasting treasure are to be discovered. Look for some tall twisty twigs that will give height to your bought flowers from the florist and you will return home exhiliarated and happy and your flower arrangements will look all the better for it.

I personally know the joy of all these discoveries, for just after the war, when my home in Kent had been bombed and I was living in one room in London, I would take a bus to the country on Sundays and come back laden with treasures for my

Made in January, although different
heathers can be obtained all year round,
this simple yet effective design was made
with stems of erica (heather) inserted into
floral foam in the top of the container. The
twisty pieces of wood were inserted first

This classic white vase holds
stems of various lilac (syringa) with ivy
berries and green *Helleborus corsicus*.
Leaves of lilac were removed to help
flower heads live longer. All held in
crumpled wire netting

flower arrangements. Most of them lasted for months, in fact I kept the tall pieces of wood for years, sometimes painting them to give them a different appearance. Wood in combination with flowers can be fascinating, provided it suits your home. Obviously a chunky piece of rough wood would not appear ideal in a formal period room, but it can look perfectly in place in a modern or country setting. So when in the country do keep your eyes open for pieces of weathered wood. If they do not present the exact shape you think you need, try screwing two or more pieces together. Scrape or brush the wood clean, so that no dust or even insects might be left in the crevices. It can then be varnished if you like, although I prefer the natural look of wood, especially the lovely grey surfaced pieces you can pick up on the shores of lakes and lochs. These pieces often get bleached by the sun and can appear very attractive when placed either at the base of a tall design or used as height with some flowers low down.

USING DRIFT WOOD

I have seen many pieces of drift wood used as main interest or focal point in various designs. It can be given various hues by polishing with different coloured shoe polishes, or sprayed with paint to give a dramatic touch to an arrangement. Just imagine the impact a design of red carnations combined with black painted wood would have. Add a large green leaf and you are almost a Piccasso with flowers. Matt or glossy paint can be used, or even a wood stain and if you wish your wood to be a lighter colour. I would suggest leaving it in a bath of diluted household bleach overnight, then left to dry after rinsing in clear water.

One more tip for colouring wood which does not conceal the texture as some paints do! Try brushing over the wood with a mixture of 1 cup of clear ammonia, 2 tablespoons of copper powder (from hardware or art shops) and 2 to 3 tablespoons of white glue. The mixture will oxidise and after the wood has dried it will take on a lovely blue/green patina.

A decade or two ago we would not have dreamt of using driftwood in our homes, but today it is very much sought after and some of the most artistic designs I have seen include it. Slabs of wood can also be used as bases for shallow containers. These can be left untouched except by the saw, or polished or just rubbed over with linseed oil which will help preserve it.

USING FRUIT

Fruit can also play a part in your arrangements, for if cleverly placed with leaves, branches or driftwood it can help to make original decorations for the home and the show. Fruit has infinite variety of shape, colour and texture and there is never a time of the year when some kind of fruit is not available and of course there can be little waste attached to such an arrangement for the fruit can always be eaten when you tire of the design. Try a bowl of green apples with white daisies tucked in between them or a pile of lemons with small bunches of violets. The violets can be placed in small bottles of water and tucked in between the fruit. Fruit can bring extra colour to an arrangement of flowers. Just imagine some purple plums or grapes at the base of pink flowers or yellow peaches with dahlias. The thought of fruit opens up a whole new field for the flower arranger. Apples, oranges and other fruits can be held together and in place with the aid of toothpicks, and if you wish to avoid round fruits from rolling about in the base of a large tray, place them on a rubber ring, or roll out a thin piece of plasticine to form a ring. Height can be given to many fruits if you pierce them with a thin stick, the type you have on toffee apples or see in pot plants, these can then be inserted at a higher level among the leaves and flowers. Yes, fruit and flowers can be fun and of course are a great aid in winter when some flowers are scarce or expensive.

FLOWERS IN HOSPITALS

There is no end to the interest in flower arranging. After nearly thirty years of intensive work with the subject, I still get excited when I see a new flower or one that I had not seen before. I get a thrill when, as recently, I was teaching in a hospital for the mentally ill, and one patient had produced a large bowl of different coloured stones that she had picked up on the shore. In between the stones she had inserted some small roots of ivy and tiny ferns. Water was added of course, but the 'picture' she presented was unique. It was *her* idea. She said she did not 'see' any flowers, but thought the stones looked attractive for some were white, some were grey and others had markings on them. The doctor wrote to me afterwards and said there had been a marked improvement in some of the patients, they found their morning walks in the grounds full of interest, and of course the hospital became the background or show place for all their various designs. They are soon

This low bowl shaped pottery container holds forsythia for height whilst the daffodils are casually grouped lower down. Tendrils of ivy, peeled of bark and bleached are intertwined and leaves cover the rim. A large pinholder held the material in place

Spring blossom, hawthorn and
pussy willow formed the triangular
outline of this design in a modern pottery
container. White iris and parrot tulips
gave the width whilst brown coloured
primulas and yellow daffodils gave central
interest. The low right swerve is *Euphorbia
wolfenii*

to hold an exhibition. We all learn from each other, so never be intimidated
thinking you do not know. You know for yourself, and what you do should be *you*.
If anyone queries it or wants to change it without requesting advice, just say 'I
like it like that'. There will come a time when *you* want to change. That is the time
to do it, when you are ready.

DRYING FLOWERS

As I have said before, the interest in flower arranging is never ending. The moment
we think we know, something else presents itself and we move on. Take the drying
of flowers for instance. This has become an absorbing interest among many men
and women. Some grow flowers specially for drying, others preserve leaves and
flowers by various methods. Not only are these dry arrangements suitable for
permanent display in various parts of the home, but they make attractive presents
or gifts for charity events.

If you have room in the garden, do sow the seed of some of the everlasting
flowers. Try the lovely pink and white *Acrocliniums,* the orange and brown
Helichrysum, rose coloured *Rhodanthe,* statice in blue, yellow, white and crimson,
and include some poppies, love-in-the-mist and honesty, for their seed heads are
so useful. Decorative grasses are also most useful, I like especially the Job's tears
and hares tail grasses, for apart from their use in dried decorations, they give a
light touch to many Christmas decorations, especially when lightly brushed over
with glue and then shaken in a bag of diamante glitter. The glitter sticks like
glittering touches of frost.

Methods of drying   All of these and many more can be grown from seed, but do
pick them before they are fully mature, and hang them upside down in small
bunches to dry. If you leave them too long in the garden they might go to seed.

Many other flowers, whether annual or perennial can be dried, by hanging them
upside down in a dry airy place. The flowers will slightly shrivel, but they will
retain their colour if kept in the dark till needed.

However, many open faced or larger flowers can be dried by the burying method.
You can use powdered borax (some mix it with alum powder) or the latest method
is to dry flowers with silica gel or one of the branded names of drying desiccants.
With this method, you should cover the base of a box or a tin with silica gel (from

Wintry silver birch twigs are inserted
in the top opening of this unusual
container and surrounded by a thin
strand of cane. One spray of yellow
chrysanthemums split into three pieces
was inserted into two further openings.
Fix five tubes together to create a home-
made version of this container

chemists or garden sundriesmen), and lay your short stemmed flowers on it.
Then with a spoon add more powder, placing it between and underneath the
petals until the whole flower is covered. Several can be dried in the same box as
long as they do not touch each other, but in this way, the flowers will retain their
three dimensional shape and their colour perfectly. About two weeks is required
for the borax method and three days for the silica gel. The borax is cheaper, but it
sometimes cakes together, whereas the silica freely flows, but both can be used
again and again. All dried flowers become brittle, so it is wise, if you need a long
stem, to insert a wire through the flower head, before drying them.

PRESERVING LEAVES
Many leaves can be preserved for winter use by the glycerine and water method.
Make a mixture of one part glycerine and two parts hot water and stand the stems
of leafy shrubs in it until the leaves turn a glossy brown. This usually takes about
two or three weeks, but one they have absorbed the mixture, they are preserved
for all time. The most popular greenery for this method is sprays of beech leaves,
but I have preserved magnolia grandiflora, berberris, eucalyptus, *Choisya ternata*,
and many many others, but do remember this method is mainly meant for the
woody stemmed shrubby leaves and not for soft stemmed leaves, such as hostas.
When preserving leaves in glycerine and water, I usually swish them through warm
water first to remove dust and then split the stem ends for easier intake of the
mixture. (It should be done whilst the sap is still rising.)

   Ferns and some other flat leaves such as virginia creeper require pressing between
blotting paper or newspaper, but the whole subject of drying and preserving
flowers and leaves is vast and obsarbing. A great deal of the fun can be had by
experimenting yourself and when finally you make an arrangement of brown
glossy leaves with beige coloured grasses and seed heads interspersed with colourful
dried gourds (grown from seed), only then will you feel the sense of achievement.
So do remember, you can (1) hang some upside down to dry, (2) dry others in
powder, (3) preserve leafy shrubs in glycerine and (4) press others between paper.

The pine was placed first, then
the leaves and finally the three yellow
Arum lilies each cut shorter than the
other to form this modern design in a
pottery container. No holder was required,
but if the first stems do not stand firm,
twist a hairpin round them and hitch this
over the rim at the back

CARE OF FRESH FLOWERS

Fresh flowers also need care if they are to give of their best when arranged. Here
are a few tips that I have found satisfactory and helpful. Whether you pick or buy
your flowers, try to get them the day before you need to display them. Then, on
returning home:

1 Recut the stem ends and leave them all in deep water overnight so that the stems
become fully charged with water. This avoids them flagging as they so often do if
put in a vase immediately from the garden.

2 Strip off the lower leaves, or those that will go below the water line, for these will
only foul the water, and leaves will often take up the water which is really deeded
by the flower head. Leaves can always be inserted separately.

3 All woody stemmed flowers, such as viburnums, lilacs, chrysanthemums, roses
and other flowering shrubs should have the stem ends split before being placed in
deep water, and of course the lower leaves removed.

4 Other soft stemmed leaves, such as hostas and sprays of young greenery should
be submerged in water to which a little sugar has been added (about a teaspoonful
to 2 pints) as this will strengthen them. This does not apply to the grey woolly
type of leaf like lambs' ears (*Stachys lanata*) as these soak up water like a sponge
and lose their pale grey appearance.

5 Always remove the white portion of the stem ends of bulbous flowers such as
tulips and daffodils as they drink only from the green portion.

6 Have tepid water in the vase before inserting the flowers, and top up each day.
Flowers are always thirsty.

7 Certain hollow stemmed flowers such as delphiniums and lupins will benefit if
the hollow stems are filled with water after cutting, then plugged with cotton wool
before being left in deep water overnight. This way sound a little fussy, but when
you can add three days to the life of your lovely tall flowers, you may think it is
worth it.

8 Many flowers, especially roses, if wilting will respond very well if the stems are
recut and split and stood in very hot water until it cools. A little sugar will help.
This does not apply to soft stemmed flowers.

9 A tablet of charcoal in the water will keep it pure. An alternative is a few spots of
clear disinfectant.

Another way of using daffodils early in the year. A branch is held on a pinholder in a tin of water standing at the right on the wooden base. The daffodils are next inserted, the holder being covered with moss. The snowdrops are held in small pots of water

10 Try to pick flowers later at night or early morning when transpiration is at its lowest. Then leave them in water either overnight or for a few hours to give them a deep drink before being used.

11 Blossoming sprays can be forced into bloom by first submerging them in warm water to swell the buds, then after splitting the stem ends, standing them in warm water in a warm room. Pick the sprays only when the buds are swollen.

The more you become interested, the more you will discuss this subject with others and the more tips you will pick up. I am always learning. I do hope you enjoy the pictures on the following pages just as much as I enjoyed making them, but I was taken aback when showing them to a temporary secretary. She said, 'I love them all, but how do you get the flowers in the vase.' Well, I did not intend this to be a 'how to do it' book, I've already covered that with step by step pictures in my book the *ABC of Flower Arranging,* but I saw her point, so here are a few more tips.

1 First, study the setting in which the flowers will be seen, ie do you want a tall arrangement for a narrow space, or a large triangular arrangement for the centre of a table placed against a wall? Do you want a low round design for an occasional table, or do you want a modern style for a contemporary setting?

2 Pick or buy accordingly.

3 When using crumpled wire netting fill the vase and allow it to reach 2 to 5 centimeters (an inch or two) above the rim. This allows you to tuck side stems through the wire and down into the water. The same applies if using one of the many floral foams that are available. These should be soaked in water until they are wet right through.

4 After preparing your vase, make your outline or shape first with the tallest, thinnest stems. Next strengthen the centre with the bigger flowers and finally fill in from the outside to the centre with the intermediate type of flowers.

5 Cut your flowers to different lengths and make sure some of the lower flowers flow forward over the rim. This will avoid a flat effect. Add leaves at the back.

6 Try to leave a space at the back into which a of water can be added each day.

7 Study other flower arrangements that you admire and try to understand how they were composed.

Hazel catkins form the height in this arrangement with daffodils and primroses. The stems were held on a pinholder in a dish of water which stood at the left of the wooden base. Moss and driftwood hid the dish

8 In nearly all good flower arrangements the stems appear to emerge from a central point which is often emphasised.

Flowers play an important role in our lives from the moment we are born until we die. Rooms are brought to life with them, hotels offer a welcome with them. Churches spread joy and goodwill with flowers, and the therapeutic value of flowers in hospitals is a well known fact. In my travels round the world I have discovered that there is no greater common denominator than flowers, for surely they are loved by all. They are not manufactured by one exclusive country, nor are they one particular person's invention or right. They are Natures gifts for everyone and are to be found in all sizes, shapes, varieties and colours in virtually every part of the world.

I am lucky to have 'found' flowers for my life's work. I hope you will make the same discovery.

Julia Clements
Chelsea
London 1976

Oasis available from florists.

28

A glass dish filled with wire netting over a pinholder is stood on this silver compote stand. A heavy hairpin fixes the grapes to the wire first and the flowers are added from the outside to the centre, where you see pink crinums and pink giraffe dahlias. Maroon atriplex is on the outside

Right White iris and freesias formed the outline of this triangular formal arrangement of spring flowers. *Thalia narcissi* were used in the centre surrounded by green *Helleborus corsicus*. The bell like blossom of *Pieris japonica* droops over the rim

An easy method of making an arrangement is to cluster flowers, I used mimosa, in the narrow neck of a bottle shaped container, adding some twisty branches of catkins flowing out at the left. The bottle was black and the base was yellow

Right   No holder was required in this narrow necked bottle shaped vase. Stems of mimosa were first inserted followed by the short stems of chrysanthemums removed from two long spray stems we buy in winter

Seven mauve alliums (onion flowers) and two *Fatzia japonica* leaves are here inserted in a green glass bottle to form the appropriate decoration for a curry party. The bulbs of alliums of various sizes should be planted in November

Right The silver tray held the candelabra standing on a large plate surrounded by wet Oasis. Into the Oasis was inserted the red carnations and greenery whilst some apples were given height by sticks, others with nuts laid at the base

Four yellow/red tulips were held firm on a pinholder with two bergenia leaves in the top of this modern pottery container. Twists of red wired sisal cord were added at the right. Sisal cord from craft shops

Right Three pink camellias and two springs of ivy are here held in a tall glass candlestick on a pinholder. To avoid the holder showing, rinse the inside of the glass with melted candlewax or paint

First nearly fill this tubular vase with crumpled paper or sand to form a false platform on which to stand the pinholder which holds the tall stem of ivy. The tulips, petals pressed back for greater effect, were inserted at different levels. Add water or stand the holder in a tin of water

Right This shallow pottery dish held a pinholder placed at the right on to which the tall stems of pussy willow were inserted. Three lily flowering tulips were placed one below the other and wood and leaves covered the holder

Here a candlestick is placed in a deep plate and surrounded with crumpled wire netting into which short heads of many spring flowers are inserted in a close cluster style. Water of course is added to the plate. The candlestick could be stood on a block to avoid the water

Right The right hand opening of this modern pottery container was filled with wet floral foam. A piece of sawn off root was laid across the rim followed by the insertion of a few pink roses. Crumpled wire netting is an alternative to floral foam

Just one flower can make a restrained looking arrangement if placed on a pinholder rising from a bowl of stones. A twisty twig gave extra height and a bergenia leaf unified the stems

Right Twisty twigs of willow (*Salix tortuosa*) formed the outline for these two Peer Gynt yellow roses. No holder was required for this simple arrangement made in a Whitefriars glass bottle

An arrangement for a confined space made with short stems of white fuji spray chrysanthemums. The cone of wet Oasis is pressed into the pale green container and the short stems inserted all round interspersed here and there with green geranium leaves. Stems of *Chlorophytum* were tied together and inserted at the top

Right Press a cone-shaped block of well soaked Oasis on to a pinholder, to avoid toppling, and stand it on a cake stand. Surround the base with lemons or apples and fill the cone with short stems of chrysanthemums, inserting parsley in the spaces. An ideal type of arrangement for a small table

Large sprays of flowering shrubs make an arrangement in themselves when used in a tall pottery container. Here *Pieris japonica* is inserted at the left whilst pink camellias are at the right. A branch, peeled of bark swerves down from the centre

Right One spray of flame coloured azalea was held on a pinholder in the cup like top of this white pottery container. Three hosta *albopicta* leaves were inserted one below the other, and wood completed this simple design

A dish filled with wet Oasis pressed on to a pinholder here holds tall stems of golden privet and yellow roses in a green straw basket lid. The roses are cut to different lengths and the stem ends split to help them last longer

Right This formal arrangement of peach/pink Fleur Cowles roses combined with stems of green *Alchemilla mollis* is made in a tall china vase. The stems are held firm in wet floral foam

A play on yellow and green is here made with a swerved branch of dark green *viburnum tinus* combined with pale green apples and yellow lemons Spotted laurel (*Aucuba*) unified the stems behind the wood and the bananas added weight at the left to balance the long stretch of the branch at right

Right This gay arrangement of pampas grass and dahlias was made in a shallow dish filled with crumpled wire netting standing on a black wooden base. Green *Agapanthus* seed heads and peppers were added for extra effect

A twisted branch of black stemmed hawthorn just bursting into pale green leaf is here held on a pinholder in a dish of water. A white china oriental ornament hides the holder, which stands on a black wooden base. Inexpensive, yet effective

Right This off centre design is made with tall fine *Campanula persicifolia* and pink and white paeonies. Touches of *Alchemilla mollis* lightened the effect. The stems were held firm in wet Oasis pressed on to a pin holder

This attractive Bohemian green glass bottle holds a tied bunch of grasses or leaves, whilst a spray of flowering broom is inserted swerving out at the left. One large anthurium leaf spreading out at the right gives visual balance. No holder required

Right Exotic anthuriums are economical in use since they last a long time in water. Here you see two bright red blooms (botanically, spathes) with two leaves dramatically displayed in a modern pottery container

This dried arrangement, is made in a block of floral foam, pressed on to a pinholder which avoids it toppling. Bulrushes and stems of wheat gave height, whilst dried fern fronds introduced curves at the sides. Poppy seed heads and clipped palmetto ferns gave central interest and glycerine preserved eucalyptus leaves flowed out low down. A piece of wood covered the holder, on the black wooden base

Right A pinholder placed in the base of the black shallow dish held these tall gladioli, followed by shorter roses and carnations in a rectangular style. Start with the leaves at the back first. The smaller flowers are alstromerias

One red poinsettia is placed at the base of the tall sprays of grevillia foliage to form this simple Christmas arrangement. Variegated holly or *Eunonymus* is placed at the back of the poinsettia all held on a Pinholder and a piece of wood covers the tin of water

Right Dried fern fronds and glycerine preserved loquat leaves form the background to the two 'flowers' made from seeds stuck into rudbeckia seedheads. The Casa Pupo blue vase was filled with Oasis which held the stems in place

This colourful pottery cockerel was used as main interest in this group of gladioli and fruit for a party. The tall gladioli were held on a pinholder in a dish of water and backed with leaves the bright red cherries gave effect

Right This tall triangular styled arrangement was made with yellow gladioli for height and eucalyptus leaves and yellow spider chrysanthemums for width. The centre was filled in with pink nerines and maroon coloured chrysanthemums

A single stem of mahonia japonica is here placed on a pinholder in a tin of water and swerved over to the left. Colourful anemones are cut short and clustered low down, whilst a small figurine is placed as though sheltering under the leaves

Right Autumn flowers are not always yellow and brown. Here you see a group of fine pink Schizostylis with maroon *Sedum spectabile* in the centre. Green hydrangeas daisy like *Dimorphotheca* and other items completed this picture made in October

A leafless twig fixed on a pinholder gives height to the spray of winter yellow chrysanthemums backed with two sprays of camellia foliage. Simple, effective and inexpensive

Right This vase was filled with crumpled wire netting which held the tall branch of witch hazel and the tassels of *Garrya eliptica* at the side. Other flowers each cut shorter are green bells of Ireland, and green *Viburnum opulus* sterile with yellow narcissi and bronze tulips